Grace: I took an old plastic bin, turned it upside down and Mum drilled some little holes in it. When you hang it over a light bulb, it sends interesting light patterns all around the room. We should put it up in the classroom!

Ms Mari: Great job. I'll have a think about that idea ... Next is Elly.

Elly: Thanks, Ms Mari. Wait until you see what I've come up with.

Elly removes the sheet from her creation.

Ms Mari: Wow, what's that?

Elly: I've made a bookshelf from two old stepladders.

Ms Mari: That's very creative. How did you do it?

Elly: I put planks of wood between the steps. Then my big brother nailed them down. It's really useful. We could put it in our reading corner.

Ms Mari: It's a very good use of materials. Well done, Elly.

Elly: Thanks, Ms Mari. I think so too!

The Upcycling Competition

A play by Cameron Macintosh

Illustrated by Dillon Naylor

CHARACTERS

Grace
Brayden
Lachie

Ms Mari: Good morning, class. Welcome to Upcycling Competition Day!

Izumi: This is the day we show how we've made something new from something old.

Ms Mari: That's right, Izumi. You will each present your upcycled creations. Then the class will vote for the winner.

Brayden: That trophy is **mine** this year!

Elly: Don't be so sure about that!

Lachie: Yes, wait until you see what I've made!

Grace: You'll all want to give up when you see **my** creation!

Ms Mari: Being a good sport is also important. Now, who would like to go first?

All: Me!

Ms Mari: I think Brayden put his hand up first. What is your upcycled creation, Brayden?

Brayden: This is my oil-tin robot toy!

Ms Mari: It looks wonderful. How did you put it together?

Brayden: I found this olive oil tin and cleaned it with a rag. Then I glued on the other tins and decorated the model to look like a robot.

Ms Mari: Good work, Brayden. You've given these tins a whole new purpose!

Brayden: Thanks, Ms Mari. That trophy is going to look great on my bookshelf at home!

1
2
3
4
5
6
7
0

Ms Mari: Our next presenter is ... Izumi.

Izumi: Well, you're all going to love what I've made. It's a kennel for my dog, made from an old computer monitor.

Ms Mari: It's very impressive. How did you make it, Izumi?

Izumi: Dad helped me remove the old computer screen. We took out everything that was inside. Then I decorated it and put in a cushion for Angus, my dog. He loves his new home! See, he's gone inside for a nap.

Ms Mari: Fantastic work, Izumi. Now it's time to hear from Grace.

Grace: Thanks, Ms Mari. I think you'll all be impressed by the lampshade I've made.

Ms Mari: I **am** impressed! Tell us how you made it.

Lachie: I've made a wind chime from some old forks and spoons I found in our shed. When the wind blows, they bump into each other and make a tinkling sound. Have a listen!

Ms Mari: It's a very pretty sound, Lachie. And it's a lovely example of upcycling.

Brayden: Well, it's not bad, Lachie, but it's not as good as my idea. My robot's really fun to play with.

Elly: My shelves deserve the prize more than that. Bookshelves that size are very expensive!

Grace: Excuse me! **My** entry is the best. How many people would think to re-use an old rubbish bin?

Izumi: Not many, but how many people bother to save computer monitors? I've made my dog very happy too.

Lachie: None of your things make pretty sounds like mine does. We all need nice sounds in our lives, don't we, Ms Mari?

Ms Mari: Settle down, everyone. It's time for the class to vote. Write down your favourite creation on a piece of paper and put it in this box. I will then count the votes and announce the winner.

Grace: Excuse me, Ms Mari! Izumi's dog just chewed my lampshade!

Ms Mari: Please put him back on his lead, Izumi.

Izumi: I can't – he's slipped out of his collar!

Brayden: He's knocked over my robot – my tins are rolling everywhere!

Elly: Now he's made a mess on my shelves! Naughty dog!

ANGUS

Lachie: Oh, no! He just leapt onto my chime and ripped some of the cutlery off!

Grace: His teeth marks have ruined my lamp!

Elly: My shelves stink! How disgusting.

Brayden: Luckily the window is open.

Izumi: Angus, look what you've done! I'm so sorry, everyone.

Ms Mari: Settle down, class. Let's forget about voting. But I have an idea to put everyone's upcycling talents to use.

Lachie: What's that, Ms Mari?

Ms Mari: Using the parts of your broken creations, I want you to work **together** to make something new and special. Do you think you can all do that?

Elly: Maybe ... but I still think I should have won the trophy.

Grace: Let's give it a try.

Brayden: I've got an idea! We could make something amazing.

Brayden whispers his idea to the group.

Lachie: Yes! We can put it outside for the whole school to enjoy.

Grace: That sounds great. Let's get to work, upcyclers!

Later in the playground

Izumi: Look what we've made, Ms Mari.

Elly: We used my stepladder.

Brayden: And some of my tins.

Grace: We've pushed the spoons through the holes in my bin ...

Lachie: ... to make perches.

Grace: It's a bird feeder! The birds love it. Look!

Ms Mari: Well done, team. You've really upcycled your upcycling!

Ms Mari: We have one last entry in the competition. That, of course, is Lachie.

Lachie: You're all going to love what I've made. But first, let's open the window and get some fresh air.

Ms Mari: Why's that, Lachie?